The Secret to Conquering FEAR

The Secret to Conquering FEAR

MIKE HERNACKI

PELICAN PUBLISHING COMPANY
Gretna 1996

Published by the Berkley Publishing Group, 1990
Published by arrangement with the author by
  Pelican Publishing Company, Inc., 1996

First Pelican edition, September 1996

The word "Pelican" and the depiction of a pelican are
trademarks of Pelican Publishing Company, Inc.,
and are registered in the U.S. Patent and Trademark Office.

Library of Congress Cataloging-in-Publication Data

Hernacki, Mike.
  The secret to conquering fear / Mike Hernacki. — 1st Pelican ed.
    p.   cm.
  Originally published: 1990.
  ISBN 1-56554-192-8 (pbk. : alk. paper)
    1. Fear.   I. Title.
  BF575.F2H47   1996
  152.4'6—dc20   96-24881
                                                           CIP

Manufactured in the United States of America

Published by Pelican Publishing Company, Inc.
1101 Monroe Street, Gretna, Louisiana 70053

TO WANDA

Contents

1

You Are What You Fear

❀

I know who you are. You're the frustrated traveler, wanting to fly off on an exciting vacation but too terrified to step onto an airplane. You're the unhappy worker, hating your job but afraid to quit. You're the lonely single person, facing an empty weekend but lacking the courage to ask someone out. You're the unsuccessful salesperson, reaching for the telephone with a trembling hand to call a prospect but giving up and reaching for your coffee instead. Inside, you feel thwarted, defeated, and small.

Yes, I know you. You're afraid of getting sick or hurt, so you don't even try to do the exciting, risky things so many other people enjoy. You're afraid of losing money, so you let yours sit in the bank, while others profit from their investments. You're afraid of speaking in front of a group, so you avoid the risky, high-profile jobs that pay other people so handsomely. You're afraid of being rejected, so you don't even ask for what you want. Every time you let the fear win, you get angrier—at yourself and at others.

I know you. You're the one who won't ride in an elevator, or climb a ladder, or learn to swim, or tell someone off, or let yourself fall in love. You're too embarrassed to admit your fears, and too frightened to face them. You're even uncomfortable reading about them right now.

Yet every moment you're alive, your life bears the imprint of your fears. What you do and fail to do, where you go and don't go, how you feel about yourself and the rest of the world, how happy or sad you are—all of these are tied directly to your fears.

You let your fears dictate your actions, limit your income, restrict your freedom, and choose your friends. In fact, your fears run your life. To a large extent, what you fear determines who you are.

A Precious Secret

Yes, I know who you are. I've met you, I've talked with you, I've worked with you. You're my friend, my relative, my neighbor. At one time or another in my life I've feared all the things mentioned above. I still fear many of them today.

Like you, I have fears of all kinds, fears that stay with me day after day. Unreasonable, groundless fears. Like you, I procrastinate, repeatedly putting off unpleasant tasks because of some vague, nameless dread. Like you, I find myself paralyzed by fear, frozen into inaction, often not knowing why.

Heaven knows I've tried to do something about my fears in the past. I've read books about the subject; I've gone to counselors. I've even tried meditation and self-hypnosis. Maybe you've tried these things, too, and found they don't work for you, either.

Right now you might be asking yourself how this book is different from all the others that have been written about fear. With all the millions of words that have been published by psychiatrists, psychologists, and other experts on this subject, how can this little paperback, written by a layman, work better for you?

This book differs from most others in several important ways. First, it doesn't try to "get to the root" of your fear. While I admit that tracking your fears to their source is ultimately a worthwhile goal, the fact is that the process is time-consuming, difficult, and usually unnecessary, if all you're trying to do is overcome a specific fear.

Instead I offer a simple principle and suggest an easy method that helps you deal—right now—with whatever fear is keeping you from getting what you want. Many books present methods that are complicated and unworkable. Not long ago, I read a book that presented a sixteen-step approach to getting rid of your fear. That's fine, but I wonder how a person, faced with a terrifying situation, palms sweating and heart racing, is going to remember sixteen steps!

Still other books and methods try to do too much. They try to rid you of all your fears and make you forget any fear you've ever known. Well, I don't think it's possible to get rid of all your fears. It may not even be worth trying. Instead I believe that all of us have a few basic fears—usually just one or two—that cause us the most harm, day in and day out. It is those few fears that this book attacks and helps you to conquer.

As I mentioned, I'm not a psychiatrist or psychologist. I had a few courses in psychology, but that was more than twenty years ago. I'm not anywhere near being an expert on the subject. But I've discovered a Secret—a simple, precious Secret you can use to overcome, and eventually conquer, your fear. It's a Secret that's so simple, you can learn it in the next few minutes. It's a Secret that's so practical, you can use it every day for the rest of your life. With this Secret you can free yourself from whatever is holding you back and open yourself to doing and having whatever you want.

Imagine what it will be like to desire something and, for the first time in your life, just go out and get it. Imagine having the courage to quit that job you hate and start an exciting new career. Imagine making dozens of sales calls in the time you used to take for one or two. What will your life look like when you're consistently able to overcome your fear of rejection and talk to anyone you want? Where will you go, what will you accomplish, how fulfilled will you be when fear is no longer in your way?

Keep these images in the back of your mind, because you'll transform them into realities just by using the Secret. There's nothing magical or miraculous about it. Actually, when you use the Secret, you'll be making just one change in your life. One simple but profound change: You'll change how you deal with fear. And when you change how you deal with fear, ultimately you change who you are.

At first you may think this Secret is too simple; you may want to dismiss it as having little value. But that's temporary. Later, as you use the Secret and come to understand it, you'll begin to see the power behind it—a power you already possess. You'll see that it's a power you've possessed all along, though you may not have realized it.

In order to learn the Secret, you must conquer one fear immediately: the fear of facing your fear. Fortunately you've already made a start. Just by picking up this book you've acknowledged that you might have a problem and might benefit by looking at it. But right now the fear of facing your fear may be back, urging you to put down the book. If you want to do that, fine. No one will care. No one but you is as concerned about your situation as you are. No one but you will be hurt if you don't do anything about it.

But if you want to conquer your fear, you must keep reading, all the way to the end. It won't take long; this is a short book. Still, you must read it all. There's only one way to accomplish that. Just do it. Now.

Fear: Your Friend and Enemy

❋

Before you can conquer fear, before you can even deal with it, you must understand what it is. I know you've experienced it; no one can possibly go through life without experiencing fear. When you were a tiny baby and your mother first put you down and walked away, you instinctively felt the danger of being alone, and so you started crying out in fear. Since then you've experienced fear countless times, in many ways. Still, you may not understand it in a way that helps you overcome it.

Fear is a feeling, an emotion. Though it's often brought on by a thought, fear is not purely thought. It doesn't exist only in your mind. Fear has a physical element to it. When fear strikes, you feel it in your body: your heartbeat quickens; your stomach tightens; your throat goes dry. If you feel it in your head, it's like a pounding or a pressure. If you feel it in your muscles, you may actually tremble or shake.

Since fear is a feeling, it's not rational or logical. And it's not entirely predictable. Something that has never scared you before might suddenly terrify you—today—for the first time in your life. By the same token, something that has always been scary might, for some unknown reason, not bother you a bit today.

Fear is always personal—that is, your fear is yours alone. It's always subjective. Have you ever noticed that you're afraid of some things that other people aren't—and vice versa? When you were in school, did you marvel at how the other kids could get up and give reports without a trace of nervousness, while you would get clammy skin and develop a stammer the moment you faced the class? On the other hand, maybe you thought nothing of scampering up a ladder to retrieve a Frisbee from a roof, while your otherwise brave friends trembled on the ground.

If someone you love is afraid of something and you're not, you can't help them by trying to adopt their fear as yours. You can understand, you can encourage, but you can't take away fear by feeling it for them. Their fears are their own, as yours are your own.

By trying to take on someone else's fears, you only make matters worse.

Some fears are universal; they're common to people everywhere. For example, no matter where you go in the world, it's hard to find anyone who isn't at least a little bit afraid of dying. But most fears are not universal. Even common ones—such as the fear of heights, of personal injury, and of losing money—affect only a small percentage of the population.

Because fear is an emotion, you can't control its onset. You can't really tell yourself, "Don't be afraid," because chances are, by the time you say those words, you're already afraid, and the words themselves are your lame effort to talk yourself out of it. Similarly, you can't order yourself to fear something. You can't really say, "Be afraid." You either fear something or you don't. To some extent the onset of your fear will always be uncontrollable. But that's not something you ought to worry about, and here's why.

When Fear Is Your Friend

The feeling called fear is a vital part of your survival mechanism. It helps to keep you alive. It's your friend and protector. Day and night, without ever taking a rest, fear is waiting on the sidelines of your emotions, ready to jump in, warn you, and help you avoid danger. When you're deeply asleep and someone makes a loud noise, what happens? You wake up with your heart pounding, all your senses alert, your muscles tensed, ready to fight with or run from whatever awakened you.

If you know that you have this mechanism and learn how to use it, you can derive great benefits from it. For example, let's say you enjoy platform diving. You are comfortable and competent from the five-meter platform, but then someone challenges you to dive from the ten-meter height. Your immediate, uncontrollable reaction is fear: a faster heartbeat, a sudden chill, an urge to withdraw. This reaction is telling you that you are being stretched beyond your "comfort zone." It's telling you to pay attention to your fear. Before trying the higher level, get some extra instruction, approach the new height with caution, take some extra time. Make your first few dives simple and safe. Soon, under the continuing protection of fear (your friend), you'll be comfortable at ten meters.

Fear can also be a source of great enjoyment. What's the big appeal of a fast roller coaster, of riding white-water rapids in a rubber raft, of hang gliding along the edge of a rocky cliff? All of these experiences carry the intense excitement that accompanies the fear of danger—real or imagined.

When Fear Is Your Enemy

Your automatic fear/survival mechanism works well—so well, in fact, that it often keeps you from doing things even when your survival isn't remotely at stake. At these times your friend can become your enemy. Here's one example.

As noted before, to some extent everyone is afraid of dying. And starvation is one of the forms of dying that people fear a great deal. This fear is so real, so intimidating, millions of people spend years working at jobs they hate, complaining every day, wishing they could work somewhere else. In my travels I've met many people with this problem, and when I've asked them why they don't quit the jobs they hate so much, they give responses that are almost ridiculous.

- "What? And starve to death?"
- "I've got a bad habit; I like to eat."
- "I'd quit, but I've got a family to feed."

You've heard these old excuses. You may even have used them yourself, without really thinking about them.

The truth is, for someone who is thinking

about quitting a job, starvation is not the real danger. At that point it's probably not even a remote danger. The levels of descent between quitting a job and starving to death are so numerous that a person would need to suffer an unlikely series of major misfortunes in order to have it happen.

What people really fear is the *insecurity* that comes with quitting a job they're sure of. This insecurity is so frightening that against all reason, even though their survival isn't then at stake, millions of people continue to show up at places they don't want to be, doing work they despise. That's how strong fear is. That's how much a part of the survival mechanism it is.

Here's another example. Centuries ago, when people lived in tribes and were exposed to such hazards as wild animals and violent weather, it was extremely dangerous to be rejected by the other members of the tribe. A number of scientists who have studied this period of history believe that for these people, rejection by others was about the same as a sentence of death, since it was almost impossible for one person to survive alone in the vast, hostile wilderness.

That was many, many centuries ago. Yet the fear of rejection is still so much a part of our survival instinct that today, a salesperson with a full stomach and money in the bank, sitting in a comfortable office, wearing a tailored suit, will tremble with fear when reaching for the phone to make a "cold call" on a would-be prospect. The fear of rejection is so great, the salesperson will hesitate to call someone miles away who cannot possibly do the caller any harm by rejecting the sales effort.

Fear can also be your enemy when it paralyzes you in situations that call for action. One such situation is public speaking, which people regularly rank as their most dreaded fear. In some surveys, public speaking is rated even scarier than dying. Remember, rejection by the tribe is a deep-seated fear that we all inherit from our earliest ancestors. Seldom are you confronted with this fear more directly than when you're unexpectedly called upon to stand up alone in front of a large group of people who are all facing (that is, positioned *against*) you.

At such times your fear/survival instinct, triggered by that ancient danger, turns your tongue into lead and your knees into jelly. Afraid of making a fool of yourself, of being laughed at by the group, you stand there paralyzed—and your worst fears are realized. At those times you need to override that instinct and *act*. You need to recognize the fear as your enemy and conquer it.

So we see that fear is a friend, protecting us from danger, literally saving our lives every day. We see that fear is an automatic, efficient part of our survival instinct, so automatic and so efficient that it works even when there is no reason for it to do so. And when it does, this useless fear becomes our enemy, keeping us from having what we want, from enjoying our lives to the fullest.

3

❋

Fear Cannot Be Eliminated, But It Can Be Conquered

＊

As I'm writing this, Bob Hope, the entertainer, is in his mid-eighties, healthy and still working. He has been entertaining for well over seventy years—longer than most people live. He has played to audiences of millions, under all conditions, in dozens of countries all over the world.

You would think that someone who is as seasoned a professional as he is would have gotten rid of his fear of facing an audience long ago. You would think that "stage fright" is for the novice, not for someone who has made his living on the stage for more than seven decades.

Yet Bob Hope has admitted a number of times that before every performance, he still gets scared. He still feels those familiar butterflies and still has those few anxious moments before he's introduced. The fear doesn't dissipate until he walks out onto the stage, says his first line, and gets the show rolling. After more than seventy years, the fear is still there.

At first glance actress Kim Basinger would seem to be someone who has little to be afraid of. She is beautiful, talented, and successful. She has starred in a number of high-grossing movies. Before that, she was a well-paid, much-sought-after model. Yet she admits that she's lived a life of fear.

"I had a lot of fears when I was a kid," she told Dotson Rader for *Parade* magazine (October 23, 1988). "Fear was a great friend of mine." Basinger went on to explain how these fears stayed with her all her life, growing up with her until she actually had a fear of fear.

When asked if she is still frightened today, she shook her head, sucked in her breath, and said, "I have great fear."

I'm sure you can find dozens, even hundreds, of people like Bob Hope and Kim Basinger. These are but two examples that I've chosen to make a point. The point is, you'll never be rid of fear. It's a gut feeling; it's part of your survival instinct; it's part of *you*. That's why, for most people, efforts to rid themselves of fear are futile.

In fact, trying to eliminate fear from your life might not even be a good idea. If you want to be courageous, you'll *need* fear. You can't do without it. Mark Twain said, "Courage is resistance to fear, mastery of fear—not absence of fear." So don't run from fear, welcome it. Embrace it. You might as well. It'll be with you till the day you die.

Even so, most of us shun the experience of fear because it's so unpleasant. But unpleasant as this emotion can be, it does have beneficial aspects. For example, let's say you fear having your house broken into at night. This fear might cause you to install security locks on your doors and windows and to check these locks when you leave the house or turn in for the night. These measures are a good idea and may keep you from harm that you might suffer if you weren't so fearful.

Fear can benefit you in more positive ways as well. Suppose you make your living by selling a product. You've been at it a long time, have an established clientele, and make a comfortable living. About the only time you feel fear on the job is when you're "stretching" yourself: calling on a new prospect; introducing a new product; expanding into a new and unfamiliar territory.

For you, then, fear can be an internal measure of how much you're growing. If you're driving to work one Monday morning and realize that nothing on your schedule is making your stomach tighten or your heart quicken, it could be a sign that you're growing stale, or at least complacent. That day you might want to schedule a particularly challenging task just to get your adrenaline flowing and your mind working. This can benefit you in many ways. Besides sharpening your skills, it may land you a new client or enable you to get the jump on your competitors.

By allowing your fears to exist rather than trying to eliminate them, you have helped yourself in ways that might not have been possible without the fear.

Even if you know that fear cannot be eliminated, you may still have a problem—the "fear of fear" Kim Basinger talked about. If you're afraid of fear, or at least regard it as so unpleasant that you avoid it at all costs, you need to change the way you look at fear.

You, like so many others, may be looking at fear as one big, ugly, nameless thing, and you quake at the thought of it. If so, you can benefit from thinking of fear as coming in many different types, not all of which are undesirable. In *Breaking Through: Freeing Yourself from Fear, Helplessness, and Depression*, Judith Asher Miller goes so far as to name 11 types of what she calls "Paleo-Fears" (the kind we inherit from our ancient ancestors) and no less than 108 "Cerebro-Fears" (the products of the cerebral cortex, in our brain).

Once you take something apart in this way

and chop it up into little bits, it becomes a lot more manageable. It becomes *beatable.* And that's what we're after in this book. We're not out to eliminate fear; that's impossible. We're out to conquer it, and we will.

A man I used to work for quit smoking cigarettes after having been a three-pack-a-day puffer for more than thirty years. At the time I was a smoker and had unsuccessfully tried to quit dozens of times. When I saw that he had quit, even though his habit was much stronger and more ingrained than mine, I was anxious to find out how he had done it. I hoped that if I could just learn his secret, I, too, might be able to quit once and for all. So I asked him how he did it.

He leaned back in his chair, smiled, and said, "No big secret, really. One day, after coughing my lungs out for about ten minutes, I picked up my pack of cigarettes, took one out, looked at it, and said, 'Okay, you little devil, who's in charge of my life, you or me?' Right at that moment I realized that here I was, a 165-pound, 52-year-old man with a college education and a successful business—and I'm letting a little tube of paper stuffed with tobacco run my life. I realized how ridiculous that was and that the only way I'd ever beat those cigarettes would be if I saw myself as bigger than they are. I had to see myself as being in control of my life, not them. Once I had changed the way I looked at the situation, quitting came quite easily."

His words had a profound effect on me. Soon I, too, had quit smoking in the same way.

It's precisely this type of mental process that I recommend you use in handling your fear. The longer you live with a particular type of fear, the bigger it seems to become. Like a bad habit, it gets stronger the more often it's reinforced. In time you see yourself as totally helpless in the face of it.

But the truth is, *you* are always bigger and always stronger than any single fear you might have. Just like the fed-up smoker said, *you* are the one who rightfully should control your life, not something that's lesser than you. If right now your fear seems unbeatable, that's just an illusion you've created by allowing it to be reinforced too many times.

Before you can conquer a single fear, you must see yourself as being in charge of it— because you are. I'm not talking about the instinctive, automatic onset of fear we saw in Chapter 2. That type of initial reaction is largely uncontrollable. Here we're talking about what happens to that fear once it surfaces. At this point you *can* exert control over your fear. When you give up control and let the fear beat you, it's *your* decision, *your*

doing. The decision to change it, the decision to take control, must be yours also.
Once you make that decision, you, like the
ex-smoker, will find that the rest comes rel-
atively easily. When I followed my ex-boss's
lead, I was surprised how easy it could be to
quit smoking.

Once you've acknowledged that you're in
control and that you are larger and stronger
than any of your fears, you still may not
want to defeat all the fears you have. That's
okay. For one thing, not all fears are harm-
ful, as we've seen. For another, not all fears
are equally important and deserving of your
time or attention. So you can make a very
good argument for becoming selective in
your approach to conquering fear.

For you, the strategy "Divide and conquer" has real merit. If you follow the principles of this book, though, "Select and
conquer" will more accurately describe your
approach. And as thousands of others before
you have proven, it's an approach that
works.

When Fear Is Not a Problem

※

As you've been reading about the idea of dividing and classifying your fears, I'm sure you've been sorting out your own fears and making preliminary judgments about them—how strong they are, how much you want to go after them, and the like.

In doing that, sooner or later you're going to come to the conclusion that the experience of fear, by itself, isn't necessarily a *problem*. And when a fear is real but isn't a problem, you really don't need to do anything about it. Of course, this is just common sense, but many people go through life gnawing at themselves, wishing they were rid of a fear that's not really a problem.

A fear *can* be a problem, though, and when it is, you should know it, because that's a fear you'll want to conquer eventually. I've discovered an easy test that'll help you find out if a particular fear is a problem for you. Here's the test.

Think of something you want—a new job, a nicer place to live, a rewarding relationship, a new car, a vacation—anything you don't now have. Next ask yourself if you're afraid of something that is standing between you and your having that item. If the answer is yes, that is, if you don't have it because of something you fear, ask a second question: "Do I want it so badly, it bothers me that the fear is in the way of my having it?" If the answer to this question is yes, then you *do* have a problem with the fear. If the answer is no, then you have the fear, but you don't have a *problem* with it. This is an important distinction.

Let me illustrate with an example from my own experience. I've been told that downhill skiing can be great fun. I know people who train for months, then travel thousands of miles and spend thousands of dollars just to enjoy the feeling of whooshing down a snowy mountainside on two thin pieces of waxed wood (or whatever skis are made of these days).

I, too, would like to enjoy that feeling, but there's something standing in my way. I'm afraid of falling down and breaking a leg or crashing into a tree and cracking my head open. I admit it; I'm afraid of those things. I agree with Erma Bombeck, who says she can't get too excited about a sport that has an ambulance at the finish line.

Yet I know my fear is irrational, because every year millions of people all over the world spend months skiing and never even sprain a finger. Children ski and grow up with all their limbs intact. Even so, my fear is definitely there, and it's definitely standing in the way of my experiencing all the enjoyable sensations that downhill skiing could afford me.

Now, here comes the real test: Do I want those sensations so much, it *bothers* me that my fear is in the way of my having them? No, it doesn't bother me a bit. I enjoy a full, exciting life. I sail on the ocean, I ride motorcycles, I even go cross-country skiing now and then. I avail myself of many marvelous sensations, some of which involve a lot of fear, but I handle all the fear they produce. I confess that I have a fear of downhill skiing, but I firmly insist that I don't have a *problem* with that fear. It doesn't bother me. I don't think about skiing, I don't miss it, I don't care about it. Yes, I'm afraid of it, but I merely accept that particular fear and get on with my life.

The message in my little confession is this: If you want something and you're afraid to go get it, don't immediately assume your fear is a problem. Don't assume that it's keeping you from leading your life the way you want to. Instead, put it to my little test. If you don't want that item badly enough to be bothered by not having it, then your fear is *not* a problem. If your fear is not a problem, then there's no point in going around apologizing for it, covering it up, or feeling guilty about it. When you do those things, you just make yourself feel miserable—and you don't come any closer to conquering the fear.

Instead, give yourself permission to have your "no-problem" fears. Suspend judgment on yourself. After all, you no doubt overcome other fears, and do it quite capably. There are probably people who do the thing you fear but are afraid to do other things, things you handle well. Maybe you're terrified of meeting new people at parties, but you can bravely take the podium at a large gathering and talk off-the-cuff. Others, who always seem to be the life of the party, may faint at the thought of giving a speech.

The fact that you're unable to face some fears does not detract one bit from you as a person. You're valuable, capable, and competent. You're as good as the next person. Just accept your "no-problem" fears and live with them. Allow yourself to be complete, actualized, and fulfilled—fears and all. When you do, you'll eliminate a lot of guilt and wasted energy. You'll actually live a happier life. And you'll free yourself to deal with another, far more important kind of situation.

When Fear Is a Problem

✿

When dealing with an enemy of any kind, it's not wise to attack your entire opposition all at once. You must decide what part of your enemy presents the greatest threat and concentrate your attack there. If you're able to do what was suggested in the previous chapter, you have learned to not attack your "no-problem" fears. By leaving them alone, you free yourself and all your resources to deal with the "problem" fears, the ones that you ought to be attacking. The same test we applied in the previous chapter will help you to identify the "problem" fears just as easily.

Going back to my example, let's say the circumstances change. Let's say I move to a region where downhill skiing is a dominant pastime. Let's say I make friends with people who are avid skiers and who repeatedly invite me along, assuring me that my fears are groundless and that the enjoyment of skiing is worth the risk. Suppose I see them repeatedly coming back from ski trips, uninjured and raving about how much fun they've just had.

Under these new circumstances it's possible that my desire to experience downhill skiing will increase to the point where my fear of it will begin to bother me. When that happens, I'll not only have the fear, but I'll also have a *problem* with the fear. I'll be facing a fear that needs to be dealt with.

Putting this new situation to the test, I first ask myself, "Is there something I want that fear is keeping me from?" Answer: Yes, I want to go downhill skiing. Next I ask, "Do I want to go skiing so badly, it bothers me that the fear is in the way?" The new answer is also yes, and so I've identified a fear I must conquer if I'm to live my life the way I want to live it. I need The Secret to Conquering Fear.

A friend of mine was reading the first draft of this book, and when he came to this section, he said, "Here's where your theory about fear breaks down. If your readers are afraid of something but just don't want to deal with it, they've just been handed an easy way out. They can just say, 'I don't really want what's on the other side of my fear, so

I don't have a problem.' Or they can say, 'I *do* want what's on the other side of my fear, but it doesn't really bother me, so I don't have a problem, either.' "

At first that observation bothered me. Rather than helping people conquer their fears, I thought, maybe I'm just giving them an easy way to rationalize not going after what they really want.

But after I pondered this awhile, I realized that each person, deep down, *knows* when something is a problem and when it's not. Deep down, you *know* when you're lying to yourself about what you want. If you want to use this "no-problem" theory of fears as a means of escape, you will. But if something inside you demands that you face your fear and conquer it, sooner or later the rationalizing will end—and you'll respond to that inner demand. I suspect that part of the reason you're reading this book right now is that you know the time has come for you to stop avoiding fears you've been carrying around much too long already. You know it's time to start dealing with those fears.

Yet in order to deal with your fear properly, you must first recognize one important truth: that *you* are the source of your fear. No matter how inherently terrifying that thing you fear is, the source of the fear is you and you alone.

If you're like most people, you find that

statement a little hard to swallow. Let's look at it more closely.

Suppose you live in a big city, in a high-crime neighborhood, and your biggest fear is going out alone at night. You're not proud of your fear, but you believe it's justified. "Everyone in this neighborhood's afraid to go out at night," you explain. "The crime statistics don't lie. *I'm* not the source of my fear, the street criminals are."

Well, maybe. Now suppose one night you're getting ready to go to sleep and you discover that the batteries in your alarm clock have gone dead. You have an important meeting early the next morning, and being a heavy sleeper, you just know you'll oversleep without that alarm. A few blocks away is an all-night convenience store that always carries batteries. The moment you think about going to that store, you feel the fear. Wildly your mind races through a grim scenario in which you go out for the batteries, get mugged, and suffer terrible pain.

But hold on. At the time you're feeling that fear you're in no actual danger. At that moment there may not be any street criminals within miles of the route you plan to take to the store. The source of your fear is not out there on the street. The source of your fear does not even exist. But your *fear* exists; it's real. So the only place that it can have originated is within you.

Take any fear you have—no matter how universal it is, no matter how much outside yourself it appears to be—subject it to the same analysis, and inevitably you'll conclude that *you* are the source of all your fear. But don't be discouraged by this conclusion. As long as you think the source of your fear is outside yourself, the fear will always be beyond your control. As long as you think the source of your fear is someone else, that person will always control a certain part of your life.

On the other hand, once you recognize that you are the source of your fear, you can then see yourself as capable of conquering the fear. All you need is a burning desire to be rid of the fear, and some sort of method for doing it.

You'll find that the hardest part of conquering fear is admitting that you—and no one or nothing else—are the source of your fears. The reason for this is simple: As long as you put the source of your fear outside yourself, you always have an excuse for not dealing with it. But once you're completely honest with yourself, once you recognize that *you* are the source, your excuse is gone, and you *must* deal with the fear. And heaven knows you don't want to. You'd rather continue to avoid the situation or the person that scares you.

You'll let this state of affairs continue, unless or until it gets to the point where you want something very much and the fear is in the way. Then it will really help to see yourself as the source of the fear. Because at that point, you can say, "This is my fear. I've created it, I'm hanging on to it, and now I'm going to beat it." If you don't recognize yourself as the source of the fear, you can never say those words. And you won't ever conquer anything you fear.

But that's not the case. Now you *know* you're in charge. Now you're ready.

6

The Key: Your Burning Desire

❀

A few pages back I mentioned that when you put your fears to my little two-part test, you'll know, deep down inside, if you really have a problem with your fear. You might be able to kid yourself for a while, but eventually you'll have to admit that you want something so much, it bothers you not to have it.

The internal demand that lets you know you have a problem with fear is called a *burning desire*. It's a feeling of wanting that's so intense, you find it hard to be comfortable until you get what you want—until you get what's on the other side of the fear.

To make this concept more real, let's paint a mental picture. Imagine yourself on the bank of a wide, swiftly flowing river. On the other side of this river is the thing you desire. The river itself is your fear. To get to the object of your desire, you have to risk whatever dangers the river may represent to you. Now ask yourself: Can I comfortably spend the rest of my days on this side of the river, giving little thought to what's on the other side? Or will it bother me that the thing I want is not mine?

I have a friend who once worked as a quality-control inspector in a large manufacturing plant. James's job was close to ideal: good pay, regular hours, great benefits, and a lucrative pension plan. But James had a little problem. He felt he wasn't making enough of a contribution to society. He wanted to become a police officer. When the thought of quitting his job and starting anew first occurred to him, he experienced a great many fears, not the least of which were the fears of losing money and of being injured. So he dismissed the idea and just kept working at the plant.

But James's desire to become a police officer just would not leave him alone. Every time he went to work, he imagined what life would be like if he were putting on a uniform and reporting to the precinct instead. He had many long talks with his wife, who was fearful of the economic hardships that would follow the job change and of the possibility that her husband would go to work one day and never come back.

James lived with his fear—and his desire—

for several years. Hundreds of times he told himself that his job didn't really bother him that much, that he didn't need to go out and be a crusader for justice. His nice, safe inspector job made more sense and paid more money.

Then one day the desire won out. James woke up, dressed for work, got into his car, and drove over to the police recruiting station to pick up an application. He's been a police officer—and loving it—for many years now. With promotions and overtime he's managed to make nearly as much money as he did in the factory.

If you have a burning desire for something, it doesn't matter how often you say, "I really don't want that. I don't have a problem." The desire is stronger than any fear. Eventually the desire will win. Eventually you'll stop lying to yourself. Like James, you'll admit to your burning desire. When you do, the fear will come back. And you'll have a decision to make.

7

To Deal With Fear or Not

❋

To hear people talk, you would think that they are prisoners in their own homes and workplaces.

- "I'd love to change jobs, but I can't. At my age, and with my training, I'm stuck here."
- "My fondest dream is to go trekking in Nepal. But I might as well forget about it. My wife will never let me go."
- "I know I'd make a lot more money in sales, but I just wouldn't be able to handle the rejection. I can't help it, that's just the way I am."

These statements are all alike in one respect: None of them contain a speck of truth. In truth, no one who lives and works in a "free" country is stuck in a particular job.

No one is completely bound by their spouse's desires. No one is incapable of changing the way they handle rejection.

No matter what your circumstances, you always have a choice. In some societies the law will limit your choices, but for nearly everyone in a nontotalitarian country, the real choices are many and varied. So if you've been using the excuse that you have no choice, it's time to abandon it. Deep down, you know it's a lie.

Thus, when your fear emerges, and you have a problem with it, you have a choice: You can deal with it or not. You can jump into the river that separates you from the thing you want or stay where you are. Each choice has consequences. Each is going to affect your life in some way. Let's look at what happens to you in each case.

If a fear bothers you, and you refuse to deal with it, it doesn't just disappear. As you have already learned, the very opposite happens. The fear lingers. It reappears again and again. It gets bigger, stronger, and more ominous every time you're forced to look at it. What began as a small, bothersome fear grows into a full-sized phobia that haunts you with increasing tenacity until it eventually begins to run your life. More and more, your efforts are directed toward avoiding that fear. Ultimately it becomes what your life is all about. As the biblical story of Job illustrates, that

which you fear most indeed comes upon
you—with growing force and regularity.

I know a woman who, since her childhood, has had a small, unattractive blemish
on the side of her face. When she was a little
girl, the other children made fun of her ap-
pearance, and this caused her to become
afraid of dealing with people, especially
strangers. So she avoided people, keeping
more and more to herself as the years went
by. Naturally her anxiety about dealing with
people increased. In reaction to this anxiety,
she began to overeat, and her heaviness made
her even more unattractive.

This pattern has gone on for years, and today, obese and reclusive, this unfortunate
woman lives in almost constant terror of in-
teraction with people, even on the most ca-
sual level. Avoiding contact with "the
world" has become the preoccupation of her
life. She works at a job in which her inter-
action with people is limited to letters and
telephone calls. She goes out of her way to
walk on uncrowded streets. She shops by
mail order. When she does go to a store, it's
at odd hours, when few people are likely to
be shopping. One day I happened to be on
the elevator in her building when the door
opened, and there she was, waiting to step
on. I hadn't seen her in years and was truly
delighted to run into her. "Celia," I said with
a smile, "how nice to see you."

Her eyes widened, she blushed, and said, "I must look a fright." She stepped back, let the elevator doors close, and left me standing there with my mouth open.

This woman's fear runs her life. Sadly, it's a fear that started out quite small, compared to the monster phobia that imprisons her today. We can't know how difficult or how easy it might have been for this woman to conquer her fear much earlier, but we can see the disastrous consequences of her avoiding it.

My mother had a longtime friend who sustained heavy financial losses during the Great Depression. This man had been traumatized when he went to draw his money out of the bank and learned that the bank had failed and his money was lost. His stockbroker did not survive the Crash, and so his investments disappeared too.

From that time on, this man was fearful of trusting anyone with his money. Despite the guarantees of FDIC insurance, he no longer believed in banks, so he kept his savings hidden in his home. Despite the large number of new laws regulating the securities industry, he refused to make investments, so his capital didn't grow. In time this fear of loss began to consume him. Fearful of having his money stolen, he wouldn't leave his house. Afraid of being left without money, as he had been in 1929, he wouldn't buy anything that he didn't absolutely need. After he died, alone and miserable, the police broke into his apartment and found cans, boxes, and yes, even his mattress, stuffed with money.

True, his fear kept him from losing his money, but considering how much it benefited him, he might as well have been without money all those years.

These are just a few examples from my experience. I'm sure you can provide more from the lives of people you know. Maybe you, yourself, are such an example. If so, you know what happens when you choose not to deal with a particular fear. When you make that choice, your life becomes limited—narrowed—to that extent. The next fear to come along narrows it even more. Eventually, as with the people in my examples, fear pervades everything. By avoiding fear you've strengthened and solidified it. Through your own choice you've given your fear control over your life.

On the other hand, when you face a fear and deal with it, you stand a good chance of overcoming it. When you overcome it, chances are it will diminish in strength. Overcome it often enough and you can conquer it forever.

When I was in college, I had a good friend, Ted, who had suffered from a crippling childhood disease. At eighteen, he was bright and personable, but his body was permanently disfigured. Like the woman in the earlier example, he could have used his disfigurement as an excuse for not having contact with people, and certainly as a way of avoiding asking girls out. But not Ted. He had a girlfriend at another college and he dated actively at his own. One evening, after we'd shared a few beers, I asked him why he wasn't afraid of asking good-looking coeds to go out with him.

"Not afraid? Are you kidding? Don't you think that, with the way I look, I'm not afraid of approaching some campus beauty queen? I'm scared out of my mind."

"But that doesn't stop you. Why not?"

"Mike, I decided a long time ago that I wasn't going to let this damned handicap stop me from living my life. I realized that if I wanted to do something, no matter how much it scared me, I always had a choice— to do it or not. I haven't always exercised it, but I've always remembered I do have that choice."

Last I heard, Ted was married to a lovely woman, had three teenage children, and was an executive with a large newspaper. The lesson he taught me was that, no matter how difficult or intimidating something looks, we always have a choice—to attempt it or not. No matter how ingrained a habit may be, we always have a choice—to continue it or not. So the next time you're tempted to say, "I can't help it," remember the lesson that marvelous handicapped teenager taught us all.

By choosing to overcome your fear, you're exercising control over it—and so, we're back to the idea of control again. This idea is worth looking at more closely, because with fear, control is a very important factor. A considerable body of evidence bears this out.

In a series of studies carried out at Yale University in 1968, psychologist Jay Weiss gave one group of laboratory rats the opportunity to learn responses that would enable them to avoid and sometimes escape painful electric shocks. A different group of rats received the same amount of shock but could do nothing about it.

The group that was trained to perform the responses developed far fewer stress ulcers than did the group that was untrained, even though the shocks were the same. Clearly the ability of the animals to control a fearful situation lessened the amount of fear and stress associated with it.

That's fine for rats, but what about humans? Another study, conducted on men at the State University of New York in 1970, showed that simply *believing* we have control—even when we don't—markedly reduces fear and stress. In the study, researchers subjected two groups of men to electric shocks. The men in one group were told that they could reduce the shocks by pulling a switch. The men in the other group were told that the shocks would come, but that there was nothing they could do about them. Both groups actually received the same shocks. Result: The men who *believed* they could control the shocks felt less fear and less pain, even though the voltage was identical.

This doesn't mean that simply by taking control you can eliminate fear of all types from your life. We've already seen why this can't be so. Instead, when you deal with—and conquer—a certain fear, you move beyond it. You move to another level of existence. At this level you may encounter new fears, but you'll be able to deal with them in ways you could not have imagined before. Once you've gotten over your fear of diving from the ten-meter board, the fifteen-meter height may still intimidate you, but you're being intimidated at the new level. The ten-meter will never bother you in the same way it did when you first sought to conquer it. Every time you deal with fear, your life expands rather than contracts. It widens rather than narrows.

You become more alive, more aware, more powerful as a person.

So you can see how desirable it is to deal with—and eventually conquer—your fear. To do that, all you need is the Secret. And here it is.

A Secret, a Principle, a Process

Unfortunately most people go through life as victims of their fears, not knowing there's a Secret to Conquering Fear. The Secret is so simple and plain that when they read or hear it, they reject it as not being profound enough. They say, "That can't be it," overlooking the fact that often the simplest ideas are the most profound.

This particular Secret is so simple, I can give it to you in just nine words:

To conquer fear, act as if it isn't there.

Does this sound too simple, too pat? Perhaps, but there's more to it than is immediately apparent. The Secret is built on a solid principle, and it works through a process that's as effective as anything you've ever

tried before. Let's look at these two ele-
ments, the principle and the process, one at
a time.

The Principle of "Act as If"

A fundamental fact of life is that things
are the way they are, and things are not the
way they're not. No matter how much you
want or wish things to be different, the truth
is they're not different. They simply are the
way they are.

If, for example, you're afraid of speaking
in front of a group, that's the way you are.
At this moment, right now, things cannot be
any different. To maintain a healthy and productive view of the world, you *must* accept
that things are the way they are. Many people
make the mistake of refusing to accept this
fact. In other words, they deny reality—and
in so doing, they make it impossible for
themselves to deal with that reality.

I know a couple that has been engaged for
seven years. They both agree that they
should have gotten married by now, but they
can't bring themselves to do it. Their problem is that they appear to be perfectly suited
to each other, while in reality, they're not.

They have similar family backgrounds,
about the same amount of education, and

they share a wide range of interests. They work in the same field. They socialize with the same people. All their friends say that theirs is a match made in heaven. Everything about these two people looks right, except for one thing: They're just not right for each other. Whenever they spend a good deal of time together, they quarrel. Whenever they try to make plans, they can't agree, so the plans are put on hold.

Unfortunately these two people so desperately want the relationship to be right, they refuse to admit that it's just plain wrong. If they did, they could more easily see that they have several workable options. The first is the more radical. They could just shake hands, separate, and get on with their lives. The second is a little more complicated. They could confront their problems, go for counseling, and find a way to change their relationship for the better. If the counseling didn't work, they would still have the first option. In either case, they would be changing their lives in a positive way, which they are not now doing, simply because they refuse to accept things the way they are.

To avoid these kinds of situations in your life—and to help preserve your own sanity—it's important that you accept things as they are.

However, things don't necessarily have to

stay that way forever. Just because some things are a certain way at a given moment doesn't mean they can't change. Of course, there are some things that probably never will change. Horses will probably never be able to fly. Trees will probably never turn blue. Again, to maintain a healthy and productive view of life, you must accept those things that probably won't (and maybe shouldn't) change. At the same time there are a great many things in life that *can* change—and maybe should. In this category are many of the conditions, circumstances, and attitudes that make up your life.

How can we tell the difference between things we can change and those we can't? I'm afraid there's no simple answer to that question. Generally you might find it helpful to follow this line of reasoning. If the situation that's troubling you depends on how you think, what you say or what you do, then it's something you can change. If, on the other hand, there's little or nothing you can think, say, or do to affect the situation, then you're probably better off not trying.

When you were a child, you may have been terrified by thunder. That's understandable. In fact, no matter how old you are, you may still find thunder unsettling. Unfortunately there's nothing—absolutely nothing—you can do about thunder. But there is something you can do about your *reaction* to thunder. If you find yourself unable to go out on a rainy night simply because it's thundering, you've got a problem. The problem, however, is not the thunder itself. It's your reaction to thunder. And that's a problem you can and should be working on.

If you're five-foot-two inches tall and over the age of twenty-five, your height probably will never change. There's nothing you can do in the near future to become six feet tall, so you might as well accept your height as it is. If, however, because of your height, you're afraid to stand up and speak in public, then you're dealing with an entirely different condition. It's not a condition that you have to live with. *You* can change it. Here's how.

As a human being, you have the amazing, priceless ability to accept things as they are, while *at the same time* acting as if they're different. Even as you accept the reality that you *are* afraid of something, you can act as if you're not. Even as you accept the reality that you have *not* accomplished something, you can act as if you've already accomplished it. This is one of the most valuable tools you'll ever have at your disposal. Here's why.

I once knew a young and highly talented

golfer. Though he was only in his teens, Kevin had already decided that he wanted to become a professional. And people who saw him play agreed that he should. He handled the clubs with natural skill and grace. His swing was smooth and powerful; his putting touch was soft and accurate. If talent was all it took, Kevin had a big future.

But talent wasn't enough; he had an attitude problem. Every time things started going badly for him on the golf course, Kevin would lose patience with himself, then lose his temper, and eventually lose all control. One day a friend of mine, Terry, was playing in a foursome with Kevin, and while she was impressed with the boy's ability, she was shocked at his behavior. On the third green Kevin missed an easy putt. Furious at himself, he cursed, slammed the putter to the ground, and stalked off. Later he sliced a drive into the rough, then promptly threw his club in the same direction. Kevin's tantrums continued throughout the round, making everyone uncomfortable and spoiling their fun. When it was over, they were relieved. Kevin had done well on the scorecard—a few strokes over par. But Terry knew Kevin's game was going nowhere if he kept acting the way he did.

Later, in the parking lot, Terry took Kevin aside and asked who his favorite player was.

"Johnny Miller," Kevin replied without hesitating. "I want to play just like him when I'm a pro. I copy his approach, his swing, his putt, everything."

"Not everything," Terry said. "Have you ever seen Johnny Miller miss a putt like you did on three?"

"Sure. Not often, but he misses them."

"And when he does miss, do you see him slam the putter down and stomp around like you did out there?"

"Well, no," Kevin replied. "But he was on TV."

Terry held Kevin's shoulders and looked straight at him. "Johnny Miller's on TV because he's a pro, and he's a pro because he acts like one. If you want to be a pro, you've got to act like one right now—and I don't mean just in the way you swing. I mean in everything you do and say.

"If you want to play like Johnny Miller, then *be* Johnny Miller. Walk like him, talk like him, dress like him, act as if you are him. Of course, your natural differences will come out; you'll develop your own style. But that comes later. For now you just fool yourself into thinking you're Johnny Miller. And before long, you'll start breaking par for a living, like he does."

Though he initially chafed at this lecture, Kevin eventually took it to heart. He tried what Terry suggested. By the time he was out of his teens, he was winning important tournaments—at a younger age than his hero had. He was well on his way to being the kind of pro he had the talent to be.

When you *act as if*, something almost magical takes place: A mechanism inside you begins to make that change happen. Your actions begin to produce the result you want *as if* it were already accomplished.

Yes, positive thinking is powerful. But positive action is even more powerful. When you are fueled by the principle of *act as if*, you are powerful enough to to change anything that can be changed. You are even strong enough to conquer fear—any fear you have now, any fear you'll ever have.

At the very moment you're accepting your fear of public speaking you can act as if you had no such fear. When your name is called, you can stride purposefully to the podium with a big smile on your face, while butterflies are having a dogfight in your stomach. At the same time that you're acknowledging your fear of rejection, you can be asking your prospective customer for a large order. And while you're doing these things, you're using one of the most powerful principles ever discovered—a principle that's remaking you, even as you're using it.

That's the principle. Now for the second element, the process.

The Process of "What's Next?"

You can accomplish many things in life without specific action, but conquering fear isn't one of them. The Secret to Conquering Fear is action-oriented. It has to be; with fear, positive thinking and well-meaning words aren't enough. You must change your behavior. And by changing your behavior you *will* conquer your fear. It's inevitable.

The process that makes it work is simple. First decide what you want—that is, *exactly* what fear you'd like to conquer. Let's say you're a salesperson and you want to conquer your fear of making "cold" telephone calls to people you don't know. You want to succeed at your job. You have a *burning desire* to succeed, but you're afraid to make those calls.

Ask yourself, "If I weren't afraid to make cold calls, what's the first thing I'd do?" Answer: The first thing you'd do is pick up the phone.

That's simple enough. You've done it thousands of times. You have no fear of picking up the phone. So do it.

Now ask yourself, "If I weren't afraid, what's the *next* thing I'd do?" Answer: The next thing you'd do is dial a number.

That's simple also. You're not afraid to dial a number. Do it.

As you hear the ring and the receiver is

trembling in your hand, ask yourself, "If I weren't afraid, what's the next thing I'd do?" Answer: When someone answers, say "Hello."

By the time you've gone through that much of the process, someone probably will have answered, you'll have said hello and begun your sales talk without realizing it. If at any step along the way you find that your fear is simply too strong and you can't deal with it, just stop. For example, if you simply cannot bear the anxiety and must hang up before someone answers, then go ahead and hang up. You've lost nothing, yet at the same time you've made important progress. You've overcome your fear to the point of picking up the phone and dialing. Rather than just sitting there, sipping your coffee and staring at the phone, you've exercised some control over the fear. In a small way, as yet probably too small to see, you've also diminished the fear.

At this point in the process it's critical that you start again—to reinforce your partial victory and to forget your temporary setback. Once again ask yourself, "If I weren't afraid, what would I do?" Pick up the phone. "If I weren't afraid, what would I do next?" Dial a number. (So far you're on familiar ground. You may notice that your anxiety is already less.) As you hear the ring, ask again,

"If I weren't afraid, what would I do?" and then *do* it.

Let's try another example, the fear of flying. Suppose you want to visit Hawaii. You've heard how beautiful it is, how much fun everyone has, and how hospitable Hawaiians are. You want to go there desperately, but you've avoided it because you're afraid to fly. What do you do?

Ask yourself, "If I weren't afraid to fly and I wanted to go to Hawaii, what would I do?" Answer: You'd call a travel agent and ask about tour information. Are you afraid to do that? Of course not; you've talked to people on the phone—some of them travel agents— many times, with no ill effect. So you call. Once you've gotten all the information you want and make a decision about which tour to take, what's next? If you weren't afraid to fly, you'd call and make your reservation. That shouldn't be a problem. You've called and made reservations before—at restaurants, theaters, maybe even on trains.

By now you get the picture. Just keep asking "What's next?" until you find yourself buckled into your seat on a 747 (a very safe plane) with visions of palm trees and golden sunsets dancing in your head, even as your knuckles turn white and you tremble in mortal fear. Then, as the wheels of the giant plane leave the ground and your fear grows into the size of a basketball in your chest, you feel a new emotion—pride. You faced the fear and you conquered it!

This process is extraordinarily effective in helping people to overcome, and eventually conquer, fear. I suspect one reason it works so well is that no matter how much we fear something, when that thing is broken up into a series of harmless, manageable steps, it doesn't look so scary. Rarely do we ever fear every tiny aspect of something. But when we see it as a huge, undivided entity, our brains *trick* us into thinking we're afraid of the whole thing. And we come to irrational conclusions, such as "I'm afraid of making cold calls" or "I'm terrified of flying" or, in my case, "I'm afraid to go skiing."

Once we come to such an irrational conclusion, a major obstacle to dealing with our fear soon becomes the very act of getting started. We'll go to bizarre extremes to avoid picking up the phone: reading the paper, straightening up the desk, sharpening pencils, getting a fresh cup of coffee—anything to put off taking the first step. The process of "What's next?" simply makes getting started easier and less intimidating. It takes the fear out of the first step. And there's a bonus: Because the subsequent steps are so small and harmless, "What's next?" makes it easier for you to keep going too.

By the way, if you're the kind of person who resists facing and dealing with your fears, you have, in reading this book, already used the Secret at least once. Remember, in the beginning, I mentioned that you had to conquer one fear immediately? It was the fear of facing your fear. I advised you that there was only one way to accomplish that— by continuing to read. I told you just to do it. When you did, you used the Secret. You acted as if your fear wasn't there and kept on reading, step by step, one word, one sentence, one page at a time. And you conquered your fear. Congratulations.

See how easy?

9

How the Principle and
the Process Work Together

Quickly, let's review our basic principle: You can change your life by accepting things the way they are, while at the same time *acting as if* they were different. You can conquer your fear by accepting that you feel the fear, while at the same time *acting as if* you don't.

When you use the process of "What's next?" you're actually putting the principle to work in real-life situations. You're *acting as if* you were not afraid of the thing you're afraid to do. And when you *act as if*, something inside you automatically begins to make it so. Bit by bit, step by step, every time you apply the principle with the process, you change your life.

Is this a new idea, something I just discovered? No. Ralph Waldo Emerson, who lived more than a hundred years ago, said, "Do the thing we fear, and the death of fear is certain." And a generation ago, Dale Carnegie advised, "Do the thing you fear to do and keep on doing it . . . that is the quickest and surest way ever yet discovered to conquer fear."

But let me caution you about something. For most people the roots of fear generally go very, very deep. Psychologists and psychiatrists tell us that many of our fears originate in our early childhood and are reinforced for years and years. Often the causes of our fears become buried over time and we have no awareness of them. Don't expect the process of "What's next?" to wipe out your fears like magic. That's not what *The Secret to Conquering Fear* is all about. The Secret will enable you to do things that will get you what you want—in a reasonably short time, with relative ease. As such, it may not be as good as getting rid of the fear completely. But for right now it's plenty good enough.

For many years my sister, who lives in Michigan, has had a dear friend who lives in Texas. The two women had been neighbors back in the sixties, but because of job transfers, they now find themselves many miles apart. Even so, they keep in touch and speak on the phone often. Several times my sister has flown to Texas for weekends, but she and her friend agree the visits were too short and too scarce. Until recently her friend could not return the visits because she was afraid to fly. Because of time constraints, she was unable to drive that distance, and so she found herself frustrated, stuck, and grounded by her fear.

In 1984, I self-published a little booklet about how to overcome fear and began distributing it to a few friends and relatives. Its basic message was the same as this one. My sister sent a copy of the booklet to her friend in Texas. Before the month was out, this woman had put the principle to work, applied the process, and managed to fly to Michigan for a long, wonderful visit that she and my sister enjoyed thoroughly. For her the Secret worked—as it does for so many people. But that's not the point of this story.

My sister tells me that since her friend took that courageous, breakthrough plane ride, she has seldom, if ever, flown again. In other words, she has not gotten to the bottom of the problem. She has not worked through it and dug out the cause of her fear. For reasons only she knows, she chooses to let the fear linger. Yet by learning a simple principle and applying it to a real situation, she overcame her fear—she *conquered* it— and then went on with her life. By putting the Secret to work, she was able to achieve a desirable result—quickly, painlessly, and inexpensively. That's what you can do whenever you want to, now that you have the Secret.

One of these days you may choose to go through counseling, psychotherapy, or some other process designed to help you get to the root of your fear and be rid of it altogether. That's fine, but the process could take years, cost thousands of dollars, and cause you a great deal of pain. In the meantime you have a life to live, goals to achieve, desires to fulfill. By overcoming your fear—today—you can start to live that life, achieve those goals, and fulfill those desires. Without a therapist, without tranquilizers, without great trauma, you can *act as if* the fear is gone and get what you want.

By the way, the process I call "What's next?" is something I made up. It works for me, and it has worked for thousands of people who read the booklet that originally explained it. If it works for you, then use it. If in applying the principle you find some other process that works better, then use that one. Your intention, and the principle you employ, are far more important than any method. No matter how scientific someone says their method is, you know the truth as well as I do: Every technique works for some people and not for others.

Don't look to me or someone else for a method or a "how-to" formula that never fails. Deep down, *you* know what's best for you. No one on earth knows you better than you know yourself. Use the Secret in the way that your intuition suggests, and you'll start getting results like you've never had before.

10

Pleasant Surprises

People who use the Secret are often pleasantly surprised to learn that what they fear never happens. Those who fear rejection find that not all prospective customers reject a sales effort. Many, in fact, are polite and interested. Some are ready to buy and ask for more information. A few even buy on the first call.

Those who are afraid to ride in airplanes soon learn that despite all the terrifying headlines, airplanes seldom crash. Air travel, we're told, is far safer than any other form of transportation—certainly safer than riding in an automobile. People who fear speaking in public discover that they're almost never attacked, ridiculed, or even booed by their audiences.

Many years ago I was a major-league worrier. I worried about everything from losing my money to having my house burn down. Then one day a friend, who also happens to be professional counselor, said, "Why worry? More than ninety percent of what you're worrying about will never, ever happen." I made mental note of that and began to notice how often the things I worried about happened. I soon realized that my friend was absolutely right: Not only do the things we worry about almost never happen, they almost never even come close to happening! I seldom worry anymore.

The same thing is true of fear. Most of what we fear never happens. And a process like "What's next?" proves it—in most cases, immediately.

Another pleasant surprise takes place over a much longer period. Here's what happens: Every time you go through the steps that comprise the thing you fear, you become more familiar with them. As they become more familiar, you become more comfortable with them. In time, though the fear is still present, you're so comfortable with the steps that conquering the fear is easy. The fear itself lessens.

Through the many years I've belonged to Toastmasters (an organization of clubs in which people practice public speaking), I've met many men and women who at first were terrified to speak before the group and believed they would never get over it. One woman named Gail stands out because of a conversation I had with her a few years ago, a conversation that illustrates the point of this chapter perfectly.

I was sitting at a regular meeting in which Gail was the toastmaster. She was deftly handling the duties, introducing the speakers, making jokes with the audience, and generally guiding the meeting along at a swift, smooth pace. I admired her skill, and when the meeting ended, I made a point of telling her what a good job she had done.

"Really? I thought I'd botched it terribly," she said in her usual self-deprecating way. "Sometimes I wonder if I'm ever going to progress like the others."

"Gail," I replied, half scolding, "face the truth. Not six months ago you came to your first meeting so scared, so intimidated, you could hardly stand. When you got up and told us your name, no one could hear you. Today you ran the meeting like a pro, and soon you'll be a club officer. What happened to your fear of public speaking?"

She reacted as if I'd just shaken her out of a deep sleep. "Fear of public speaking? I don't have a—well, I did . . . well, I guess it sort of went away—while I wasn't looking."

Gail was surprised that her fear had disappeared as she faced it week after week, going to Toastmasters meetings, acting as if it weren't there, until one day it wasn't.

Mind you, this second kind of surprise can take months or years to come about. But it *will* happen. How do you know? Because of the principle of *act as if*. When you *act as if*, something inside you *automatically* makes it happen. Every time you *act as if*, you cause that something to activate. Every time you get a tiny bit closer to not being afraid. The progress might be so slight, you don't even notice it. But it's progress, nevertheless. With patience and persistence, you can actually cause your fear to go away. You get more than you expected when you first tried the Secret. Or, in the words of Henry Ford, "One of the great discoveries a man makes, one of his great surprises, is to find that he can do what he was afraid he couldn't do."

If Mr. Ford were alive today, I'm sure he'd say the same thing about Gail.

11

What to Do With the Secret

✿

Now you know the Secret to Conquering Fear. The next question is: What do you do with it? That, my friend, is entirely up to you. Some people will put down this book and forget about the whole thing. Others will try it, find that it doesn't work the first few times, and give up. Still others will try it, find that it *does* work, but won't use it again. Let's hope that you're a fourth kind of person—the kind that will use it successfully, again and again, to help yourself do and get the things you want.

Still, what you do is your business. I won't give any advice in that regard. Instead I'll briefly describe how I use the Secret, and you can start developing a workable method for yourself.

I'm going to suggest a three-stage process. Mind you, this process is entirely optional;

you don't have to employ any particular how-to method. It's also arbitrary to a certain extent; I do it my way, for no other reason than that it works for me. If something else works for you, do that instead.

The process starts when a fear materializes. Since fear is an emotion, it almost always happens by itself, in a way that I can't control. When it happens, I simply let it. I learned many years ago that there's no sense in trying to deny that a fear exists. If I try to crowd it out with other thoughts, I only delay handling it. I know that the fear will just pop up again sooner or later, and when it does, it's generally bigger and uglier. So I just let it happen.

Using an earlier example, let's say I'm invited to go skiing. Immediately the fear of being injured in a skiing accident surfaces. I've felt this fear before, so I just let it be there. I don't tell myself how silly I am, or that I have no right to feel this way. I just coexist with the fear, sitting there, uncomfortable and uncertain at stage one.

If you'll recall, I mentioned that just because a person has a fear doesn't mean he has a problem with that fear. The fear is only a problem when it keeps him from having something he really wants. This takes me to the second stage.

Next I look at what the fear is keeping me from. In this case the fear is keeping me from an enjoyable weekend in the mountains, good companionship, and all the desirable things associated with skiing. It's now time to make a decision. I must decide if I want the things on the other side of the fear badly enough to consider going after them. Do I want them so much that it bothers me not to have them? If I don't want them badly enough, fine. I simply decide not to employ the Secret.

In the case of skiing, I've gone through this many times. So far I've always decided that I didn't want to go skiing badly enough to do anything about the fear. But in other cases I've often decided that I *do* want what's on the other side of the fear—and I want it so badly, I'm really bothered by not having it. I'm bothered so much that I'm willing to consider going for it. This brings me to the next stage.

At stage three, I look at what I'm afraid of and what will happen if I act in spite of it. If the possible consequence is not *guaranteed* to seriously harm me, then I have no reason to act in spite of it. My reason, my justification, is that I really, really want what's on the other side of the fear. I have the requisite *burning desire*. And so I act. I just do it.

Here's an example. Some years ago my wife and I wanted to move from Michigan to Southern California. We had lived our entire lives in an area where the winters were bitter, the summers muggy, and the seasons in between too short. We wanted to live where we could picnic and swim outdoors all year, where we wouldn't have to shovel snow or wear big, heavy coats. We wanted to find out what the California life-style was like, firsthand.

But while the prospect of all this was tempting, it was also terrifying. We both had family, friends, and secure, high-paying jobs in Michigan. We had none of those in California. Real estate prices in San Diego, where we decided we wanted to settle, were intimidating. Jobs were hard to find. If we moved and didn't find work immediately, we could be wiped out financially.

When the fear hit us, the first thing we did was look at what the fear was keeping us from. In this case, it was keeping us from moving to San Diego and, consequently, from all the good things that we believed San Diego could offer us. We had to ask ourselves if we wanted to live in San Diego badly enough to consider going after it. We decided that yes, we did want it badly enough.

Next we looked at what we were afraid of—loneliness, insecurity, financial ruin—and what would happen if we moved, anyway. We asked ourselves, "Are we absolutely sure that we won't be able to survive in

San Diego?" The answer to that question was, of course, no. We had no family there, and only two friends, whom we hadn't seen in years. Even so, we knew that we could make friends. We might not be able to buy a house, but we could certainly afford to rent an apartment. We might not find the jobs we wanted right away, but San Diego was growing, and lower-paying jobs were available. With hard work and a little luck, we could handle the change and do well in the new city. By itself, that answer would've been enough. But we asked ourselves another question: "Even if we do go broke, or find that we're unhappy, are we absolutely sure we won't recover?" The answer to that question was also no. Plenty of people have undergone far worse hardships than we were facing and have been able to recover nicely. We had no reason to believe we couldn't do the same.

And so we put the Secret to work. Starting with the first step, we asked ourselves, "If we weren't afraid to do this, what would we do?" We did it. Step by step, we asked, "What's next?" and step by step, we went through the process of selling our home in Michigan, finding an apartment in San Diego, looking for jobs, and eventually making the move.

As we were going through this process, well-meaning friends, coworkers, and family members repeatedly reminded us how foolish we were, how much we could lose, how much we were giving up, and how dismal our prospects were. We realized, of course, that they were just vocalizing their own fears, so we paid little attention to them.

Naturally, when we got to San Diego, we had difficulties. I had to take a job paying less than half of what I'd been earning in Michigan. My wife was unable to find work at all for several months, and finally, in desperation, she took a job she really didn't want in a field she didn't like. We both missed our families, our friends, and the careers we'd left behind.

But the things we feared the most—unhappiness and financial ruin—never materialized. We've lived in San Diego since 1977, and have never been happier or more prosperous. We have many good friends, live in a house on a hill with a great view of the city and bay, and are both doing work we enjoy. Much to our delight, one of our favorite relatives moved to San Diego a few years after we did, and is happy here too.

Since we moved, we've talked to many people, back in Michigan and in other places, who've told us that they, too, would like to make such a change. When we ask why they don't do it, they confess to having the same kinds of fears we had. In questioning them further, we invariably find that they are *un-*

willing to take the *first step* toward getting what they want. They simply don't know the Secret: that in taking the first step, they've already begun to conquer their fears—and the thing they desire is already on its way to them.

By the way, my wife and I still have a very real fear of financial ruin. Maybe it's because our parents went through terrible financial difficulties—mine in the Great Depression, hers in World War II. We haven't eliminated that fear; perhaps we never will. But we did overcome it in order to get what we wanted. Since then we've come to face the fear of financial loss on several occasions. At the times we chose to deal with it, the fear was easier to handle than when we made our move. In fact, since then we've faced much larger financial risks—and when we chose to, we conquered fear at a level that was much higher than it was the first time.

And that's how we discovered what I call The Best Surprise of All.

The Best Surprise of All

❁

The best way to explain this may be by way of analogy. Think back to when you first learned a skill—let's say, arithmetic. In the beginning, as your teacher introduced new concepts, like addition, you had great difficulty with even the simplest problems. You thought and struggled and worked hard to figure out how something that looked like this—2 + 3—could be the same as something that looked like this: 5. But through patience, understanding, and repetition, your teacher got you to the point where you were comfortable working out the problem 2 + 3 = 5. Before long, you were struggling again—not with 2 + 3 = 5 but with 34 + 26 = 60. You were still working hard, you were still solving problems, but at a higher level. You kept doing that—going to higher and higher levels—until in high school you were struggling with algebra and maybe even calculus.

When you use the Secret and conquer your fear, something happens to you. You become stronger. You become larger than the fear. The fear still exists, but somehow it's less than you are. When you conquer your fear, you prepare yourself for another level, just as when you conquered single-digit addition you prepared yourself for double-digit addition. Once you're comfortable diving off the ten-meter board, you can tackle the fifteen-meter board. Once you're comfortable risking a thousand dollars, you can try risking ten thousand. And once you've risked ten thousand, you can go on to a hundred thousand.

Be aware that the Secret doesn't get rid of fear. If anything, the Secret brings fear into your life more often, and in more ways. As you conquer new fears, larger fears, more frightening fears, your life becomes wider, more interesting, more exciting than you ever dreamed. And that's the best surprise of all—when the emotion we've been taught to dread all our lives turns out to be the source of more good things than you ever thought possible.

We can't rid our lives of danger. We can't free ourselves from fear. But by using the Secret we can make our lives an exciting adventure. And if we can do that, what more could we possibly want?